Day Break Devotions

40-DAY

JOURNEY AFTER THE STORM

Vol. 1

A Sequel of Daily Healing Words for the Soul

Lawanda N. Carswell

Day Break Devotions

40-DAY JOURNEY AFTER THE STORM Vol. 1

A Sequel of Daily Healing Words for the Soul

HOV Publishing a division of HOV, LLC.
www.hovpub.com
hopeofvision@gmail.com

Cover Design: HOV Design Solutions
Editor: Carol Patterson

Write the Author Lawanda N. Carswell at:
Email: lcarswell22@yahoo.com

For more information about special discounts for bulk purchases, please contact: lcarswell22@yahoo.com.

ISBN 978-1-942871-56-9
Library of Congress Control Number: 2019936508

10 9 8 7 6 5 4 3 2 1

Printed in the United States of America

Dedication

Day Break Devotions: After the Storm is dedicated to my Lord and Savior who walked, talked, and guided me in my spiritual walk. Lord, You have seen me through trying moments and allowed me to push my way through them. I constantly read these scriptures for comfort: Matthew 6:33 "*But seek first the kingdom of God and His righteousness, and all these things shall be added to you,*" Jeremiah 29:11 *"For I know the thoughts that I think toward you, thoughts of peace and not of evil, to give you a future and a hope,*" Isaiah 40:31 *"But those who trust in the Lord will find new strength. They soar high on wings like eagles. They will run and not grow weary. They will walk and not faint,"* Psalm 23:1 "*The Lord is my shepherd: I shall not want; Psalm 23:4 "Yea, though I walk through the valley of the shadow of death I will fear no evil: for you are with me; your rod and your staff, they comfort me,"* James 4:7 *"Therefore, submit to God. Resist the devil and he will flee,"* and my favorite, Psalm 139: 13-14 "*For You formed my inward parts; You covered me in my mother's womb. I will praise You, for I am fearfully and wonderfully made. Marvelous are Your works and that my soul knows very well."*

I hold these scriptures dear in my heart for many different reasons. Lord, I could have thrown in the towel long ago, but I lifted my eyes to the hills from whence my help comes. You, Lord, have carried me over every mountain and seen me through every valley. You have bottled every tear I cried at Your throne. Each test, trial, or tribulation strengthened my weakest areas, and taught me to stand in Your word. The blessings were incredible to experience and deserve a "HALLELUJAH"!

I want to share these devotions with believers who need encouragement to strengthen their faith, trust, belief and hope in You, Lord. My hope is these devotions will provide blessed assurance when believers encounter difficult storms along their walk and that they will be encouraged to stay committed to do Your will.

Acknowledgements

My Heavenly Father gets all the recognition and praise for giving me the utensils to develop these daily messages. It's an honor and privilege to be used by You, Lord. You know what You are doing each time and I truly thank You so-o-o-o much.

Thank you, Mrs. Germaine Miller-Summers and Hope of Vision Publishing, for continuing to make it possible to print these devotions God allows me to write to share with others. I praise God for Mrs. Miller, a woman of God, who has the passion to assist individuals in bringing their visions to fruition. I thank God for you. Also, I thank God for the editor who will read each devotion to ensure each conveys a message to the reader.

My daughter, Ja'Nayla Barber, has been there every step of the way with me as I wrote, balanced motherhood, work, time to communicate with you, and be involved in your extra curriculum activities. You are my Number 1 supporter and shower me with much love. I love you, Boo, especially those fun moments of talking, laughing, and watching movies together.

Thank you to my father, Terry Carswell. I love you dearly for sharing your insights on different topics and sharing the laughter in your heart that keeps a smile on my face. Thank you for being my special critic who reviews the final product before I hand it over to be published. You're also one of my cheerleaders on the side lines. I thank God, every day for the father you are to me.

Thank you mother, Cynthia Carswell for giving me the raw, uncut truth to help me to be better as I walk this journey. You are the best mother I could have ever asked for. Thank you for also being one of my cheerleaders on the sidelines and for lifting and pumping up my spirit.

Thank you to my sister and god-sister, Sherri Carswell and Jameka Carey for all your love and support. I cherish my two little nieces, Di'Vya Iverson and Katelyn Carey for your beautiful smiles and laughter when I see both of you. I thank you all my family for your support as well.

Also, special thanks to Shanta Moore, Edward Oliver, UMBC Evangelism Ministry, UMBC Sunday School Ministry (Brother Ben Collins), Sister/Friend-Donetta Fields, Pamela Lockett, Dianna Knox Cooper, Deacon James Johnson-mentor, Syemeiko Goodrum-Johnson, LaSheika Cabiness, Treshenna Miller, Carolyn Felton, Marilyn Cotton, Rosalind Parker-Harris, UMBC Sunday School Class (25 and older women), Sister Quintella Starr, Sister Gerrie Alexandria, Pastor M. J. A. Davis, Pastor Bobby Carswell, Sr., and all angels sent by God to give me spiritual insight through teaching, talking, and testimonies about our Father's Holy Word.

Table of Content

Day 1

Witnessing Our Children's Pain

The beautiful little girl smiled widely, but her eyes revealed more hurt than an adult could imagine: A young lady who sat down with a group of girls heard the beautiful little girl speak about her father. The young lady asked, "*Do you have a close relationship with your father*?" The little girl responded with a big smile, "*No.*" The young lady asked, "*Does it bother you that you don't have a relationship with him*?"

The little girl continued to smile, but her body language and eyes spoke volumes. As the little girl talked, the young lady saw the deep scars on her heart. It touched the young lady so that she prayed as she watched and listened to her talk.

Many times, we do not pay attention to our children's silent outcries. We do not think our decisions or what we place in front them causes them confusion and pain. We want to say, "They are *children; they must be obedient to us because we are adults*." We fail to see they are people too, learning about life and the ways of this world through observing us. They listening to our words, but are watching our actions attentively, thinking: "If it's good enough for my parents to do; then we can do it too."

We must wake up to the fact our children can spiral downwards because we failed to take responsibility to acknowledge our children's pain. We can't just get ourselves all together with the Lord, and not include our children. Deuteronomy 6:6-9 states "*And these words that I command you today shall be on your heart. You shall teach them diligently to your children and shall talk of them when you sit in your house, and when you walk by the way, when you lie down, and when you rise. You shall bind them as a sign on your hand, and they shall be frontlets between your eyes. You shall write them on the door posts of your house and your gates.* Our children are precious gifts from our Father. They didn't have a say in who would be their mother or father. We must be careful of the words we speak, the actions we show, and what we force on them. Respect and obedience are reciprocal in parent and children relationships to save our children before it's too late.

Day 2

Delicate

Examine the definition of the word "*delicate.*" Consider what the word, "*delicate*" means to the young woman in this scenario:

Leah, a young lady was filing papers in a cabinet when her *delicate* eye fell in her spirit. The Holy Spirit revealed to her, "*Your delicate eye is unique, straight forward, an unexplainable to others. They will not understand the strength you have obtained. They are not going to understand your intellect when you speak. They are not going to understand your drive to excel beyond their expectations. But you must nourish your delicate eye with care. So, child you know what not to do.*" Leah had tried everything to *grab the attention of her husband, but nothing worked. She* failed to love who she was, no matter what *occurred in her marriage.*

The young lady paced back and forth, shouting in exaltation, "*Oh, my God! I thank you, Jesus for my delicate eye. I heard You loud and clear*!"

Don't try to be something you are not. It will tear you up to a point that you will question who you are. You must not forget how to love yourself, to speak up for yourself. You must not forget to stand on what you believe and feel. Do not lose the drive to push forward. It's never too late to walk in your delicate eye. Remember Psalm 139:14-16: "*I will praise You, for I am fearfully and wonderfully made. Marvelous are Your works, and that my soul knows very well. My frame was not hidden from You, when I was made in secret, and skillfully wrought in the lowest parts of earth. Your eyes saw my substance, being yet unformed, and in Your book, they all were written, the days fashioned for me, when yet there were none* of *them.*"

Embrace the exceptional and peculiar person you are. Do not allow anything to turn you from it.

Size

Do you know you cannot remain the same size as you strive to grow in the Lord? You must shave off things to reach the size you are. "*It's hard being big when littles got you; you cannot stay this size.*" Both expressions articulate this idea.

A young man in the music industry and had several number one hits. When God allow him to climb the ladder of the music world, he took everyone he knew with him. He believed if he was a success, then his friends, his family, and others should be a part of that success too. He quickly learned this wasn't a good decision; he spent his earnings keeping up a lavish lifestyle for himself and his entourage until he went bankrupt. He learned the true character of many who had been around him, that is, when that happened. He was trying to fit in, to be *normal* with everyone when he wasn't normal. He learned what God had for him was *only* for him, and in due time he saw who was suppose stay in his life. He was striving to reach higher, but because *little* attached to him, it became his downfall.

Although people did not hear new music from him, he began doing the work of the Lord and became the size God needed him to be.

Often, we don't reach the size God want us to be because we are attaching things that shouldn't be there. We think everyone is worthy or ready to go where we are going, but they are not. We keep ourselves in bondage that delays our destiny. The enemy knows what's about to take place and he tries to slow it down. We fall for the trap very easily.

God reminds us *"What's for us, is for us, and no one can take it away or slow it down. It is not tailor-made for anyone else but just for us."* It could be the next level of anointing upon our lives, or it could be a new assignment in the vineyard, or even a higher position waiting for the right time for us to take hold of it. Deuteronomy 19:8 states "*Now if the Lord your God enlarges your territory, as He swore to your ancestors, and gives you all the land He promised them.*"

We must be careful who we invite into our territory. We may need to downsize our circle to only those who truly support us in reaching our size. If we don't, we will remain the same size without growth or development. Just reflect on the young man's story.

Day 4

God's got a blessing waiting on you

The Holy Spirit led a mother and her daughter (who excited and hyped to share Bible study with her mother) to the book of Ruth. The study would help them to understand how to relate to Him before they looked at the ordinance of the Church:

Naomi's husband took her and their sons to Moab because of famine in their homeland, Bethlehem. While they were in Moab, Naomi's husband dies. Then, 10 years later, both her sons die as well, leaving her with two Moabite daughters in laws. Because Naomi felt she had nothing left in Moab, she wanted to return to Bethlehem. When she discussed her plan to return with her daughters in law, they agreed to go with her. However, Naomi felt it was selfish to ask them to leave everything they knew, to go with her, and she explained the reasons why they should return home to Moab. Orpah returned, but Ruth stayed.

Ruth saw the strength in Naomi and pledged to stay until death. Nothing Naomi could say could dissuade Ruth, so Ruth accompanied her mother in law back to her homeland. They received the favor of God because of Ruth's commitment to stay by her side. The Lord had a blessing waiting on Ruth and she walked into it which brought great prosperity for Naomi and herself. What a set up to encounter!

Many of us are about to walk into a *blessing* we've been waiting on. We have been hitting every bump, corner, and stumbling block without any explanation, but God is setting us up. We may not understand the "why" at the time, or even the reasoning behind it or that it was for our good. Our Father sometimes places obstacles in our paths, such as rejection, pain, failure, loss of a love one, single parenting, unemployed, no home, or a difficult season, to open our eyes to the bigger picture, and to move us to our future blessings. Remember Psalm 34:8 "*Oh, taste and see that the Lord is good; blessed is a man who trusts in Him.*"

If we just align ourselves with the blessing our Father has for us, we will get what's designed for us, as Ruth did, as she followed the course of His will not her own. Don't get stuck on what we lost but; rejoice in what we are gaining afterwards.

Day 5

Make Me an Example

Song lyrics can be powerful; they can resonate in our spirits, and move us into a thankful mode. "Make an Example Out of Me" by Regina Bell."

> Lord, make an example out of me.
> Let my life be used as a vessel for You.
> I'm not worthy of all You do for me.
> Ooh, Lord, I give You permission
> To make an example out of me.
> Use my hands and my speech.
> Let my soul bring praise to thee.
> Fill up my cup...fill it up...
> I'll forever lift it up...
> Ooh Lord...make an example out of me.
> Here I am broken. Here I am bended.
> Here I am begging You to make as an example out of me

The words of this song reach deep down, so we can see every instance of how God brings us out and continuously works on us. We even see the times He chastised us for wrongdoing and to correct us. Be thankful that He loves us and wipes the slate clean as we asked for forgiveness. We weep tears of joy because we know what He can do and is doing right now in our lives.

We cannot fathom the power of God until we experience it personally. We hear different testimonies and see the changes in others, but it's something special to feel His power and know deep down in your soul that imprint He leaves us with. Although we may want to go tell everyone what took place in our lives, but God will remind us to be still until the time, the season, or the opportunity comes to speak on His goodness to others. We are still going through a process to understand and to gain wisdom of His Word. When he releases us, our instructions are given clearly: "*Children, you are ready to do my work and I have given you an example to share…I can take the broken and the imperfect individuals to be faithful servants to me. And I'll get all the glory and praise.*"

"And you yourself must be an example to them by doing good works of every kind. Let everything you do reflect the integrity and seriousness of your teachings." Titus 2:7

Cherish the example He has given to us on our journey, and always have His name continuously in your mouth! He's just that magnificent and amazing!

In search of Wholeness

Leroy learned a profound lesson by searching for something he already had. Leroy was very humble and quiet young man with a love for the martial arts. His martial arts teacher taught him as much as he could in the martial arts, but there was one level he needed to reach on his own. His teacher saw the disappointment in Leroy's eyes that he musts achieve this final level on his own, and so he gave him a shiny buckle and sent him on a search for the master.

Leroy set out on his quest, but and came up with nothing. Three men he thought were masters in their establishment, were not. In fact, he found out the master he searched for didn't exist. He immediately went back to his teacher and asked: "*Why did you send me on a bogus search*?" To which the teacher replied, "*I had to give you hope in what you were looking for. But there's one place Leroy, you failed to find and search, that's within yourself.*"

Leroy seems more confused than before. He finally understood his teacher's words when he conquered his biggest fear. He achieved that final level by believing in himself and his ability to do what he had been taught.

Often we search, and search, and search for that ideal thing or person to make us whole and we fail to realize we have inside of us what is necessary to be whole. Shopping sprees should not be necessary to make us feel worthy, nor should we equate love with what someone does or seems to be. Material items such as cars, homes, or monetary to make us whole. Even fear should not bring us to a standstill or make us unable to go after what we want.

God has given us all the training and skills to be whole in everything. The distractions are from the enemy to throw us off course. Listen to the ultimate master, Jesus and believe you can reach that final level.

Psalm 27:3 states "Though a host should encamp against me, my heart shall not fear: though war should rise against me, in this [will] I [be] confident." Be confident. Stop allowing fear to cripple you. Keep your head to the sky because the sky is the limit!

League

Jackie Robinson became the first African American to play major league baseball in the United States. Robinson broke the baseball color line when Brooklyn Dodgers started him at first base on April 15, 1947. The Dodgers' playing Robinson on their team ended the racial segregation that had relegated black players to the Negros Leagues since the 1880s. Robinson was inducted into the Baseball Hall of Fame in 1962. He had an exceptional 10-year career: He was the recipient of the inaugural Major League Baseball Rookie of the Year Award in 1947; an All-Star for six conservative seasons from 1949 to 1954; and won the National League Most Valuable Player in 1949, the first black to be honored. Also, he played in six World Series and contributed to the Dodgers' World Series championship in 1955.

In 1997, MLB universally retired his uniform number "42" across all major league teams; he was the first pro athlete in any sport to be so honored. The MLB also initiated and adopted on April 15, 2004, a new tradition, "Jackie Robinson Day," where every player on every team wears the number 42 on April 15. Mr. Robinson had a great career, but he dealt with a lot of things behind the scene in regard to racism. Many times, Robinson could not stay in the hotel with his team mates; he stayed in different homes that kept a room waiting for him. He heard a lot of comments that touched him, but his response was always nonviolent during his career. Even his team mates didn't accept him at first, but the more he played baseball and maintained self-control, he gained respect from everyone. His accomplishments in the MLB, placed him in a different league, a league of his own, in which he didn't need the approval of any man, because God orchestrated the plans of Robinson's life.

We must sit alone with God and only listen to His instructions. We must observe our surroundings and remove ourselves from destructive communication. We should truly examine our lives and recognize what we have accomplished in life was God's doing, not our own. We should seek to engage with positive-minded individuals. Because we are unique and different from the world, many will not understand or even know how to take us. We should seek our purpose and call from God, take it all in, and discover that we, too, are in a different league than others around us.

Yes, others are watching but it's not our concern. Yes, others are going to say a plenty, but it's not our concern. Yes, others will try to challenge us, but it's not our concern. And yes, others will try to enter our space to be nosy, but it's not our concern. Ephesians 2:10 states, "*For we are God's masterpiece. He has created us anew in Christ Jesus, so we can do the good things He planned for us long ago.*"

Our concerns must be on our Father's will for us and nothing else. That places us in a different league with an assigned purpose.

Day 8

Jesus: A Sweet Wonder

Jesus is a sweet wonder of our souls. Every day He allows us to get up to embrace another day. Jesus is a sweet wonder. He took all our imperfections and cleaned us up, so we could become disciples to serve Him. Jesus is a sweet wonder. He accepted all our dirt and mess and casted it in the Sea of Forgiveness. Jesus is a sweet wonder. He did not once hold a grudge against us, but only waits for us to return to Him. Jesus is a sweet wonder. He's calm and patient with us, even as He sees the things we have done that were not pleasing in His eyes; He never turns His back on us. Jesus is a sweet wonder. He loves us unconditional. He died on the cross at Calvary for our sins and never said a mumbling word. Jesus is a sweet wonder.

Before starting this day, reflect upon what He has done in our lives; then repeat these words:

"Jesus, the Son of God, You are wonder of my soul. You have done so much for me that I will bless Your Holy name. Everything within me cannot stop the praise and worship because You are such a wonder in

my soul. I have a 'Yes, Lord' in my spirit to serve you in any opportunity You set up for me because You continue to remind me each day of Your goodness. Yes, Lord, I'm here and available to be used by You. Jesus, You are such a wonder in my soul and I'm going to bless Your name forever!"

New Life

When the words, "new life," dropped in her spirit a young lady went online to pull up and listen to Minister John P. Kee's song, "New Life." In Minister Kee's testimony he stated "*Last Sunday, I had the opportunity to sit down with my brother. We had a conversation that touched my life. See, my oldest brother was diagnosed with cancer. I went as a brother and preacher, but God turned that thing around.*" In the testimony Minister Kee recounts what his brother said: "*They think I'm losing my mind; they sent a therapist in my room. And the therapist said I had just so many days to live*. I replied " '*I know they are paying you to say that to me, but I am not allowing a man or uniform man to tell me how long I got to live because my life belongs to God.*'" John P. Kee stated, "*I got so filled that I turned my head, so he wouldn't see but I couldn't hold it.*" In the song, at the end of the testimony, Kee asks his brother to stand, because he was a walking miracle.

The lyrics sent chills through the young lady's body. New life is a profound gift from God. Each of us has gone before God with a desire for a fresh start. There is no better way to receive it than to rejoice, weep, and release things into the spiritual atmosphere to be worked out. Our troubled heart could be mended with a new life. Our minds, though filled with this or that, can be moved to a new way of thinking. We can be delivered, in a new life, from holding on to people or things that drag us down. Our bodies' being affected with diseases that challenge our immune systems, can be rebuilt through renewed faith in God. Through every "*it could be*" scenario, there is a chance for a new life, to receive great strength, love, and support from our Heavenly Father. John 10:10 states "*The thief cometh not, but for to steal, and to kill, and to destroy: I have come that they might have life and that they might have [it] more abundantly.*" Reach for your new life and enjoy it. He wants to give it to us.

Day 10

Full Circle

How does one position oneself to come full circle? A young lady took the time to revisit a sermon she heard the previous week. In the sermon her pastor gave an illustration of a young man who witnessed a drought within a city. He walked through the city and saw no growth, no water, no vision, and no ministry. He continued to walk until he found a place, a target point, to call to the Lord. While standing in the middle of a circle, the young man said "*I'm putting in a mandate for rain*," and started walking around the circle. The sky got dark and rain start to drop. The people who were watching rejoiced. The young man continued to walk in the circle, saying to the Lord "*I just don't want a little but a bounty of rain.*" The downpour was heavy and the people were excited about the overflow. Still, the young man walked around again in a circle. He said to the Lord, "I'm not caught up in materialistic things in life, but I'm calling for Your anointing that I may move forward in my gift." He asked God for a strong, pressed down, shaken together blessing to do his Father's will.

After reflecting upon the pastor's illustration, the young lady began to walk around in a circle with a petition to God to accelerate His plans for her as she put her trust in Him. God answered faster than she could have ever thought possible.

Although you have had a drought season, keep your boxing gloves up! Opponents may have come up against you- - - such as your finance, your children, your spouse, your siblings, your parents, your faith, your hope, and even your heart- - -, but God says," H*ow long are you going to keep holding on to that drought? Do you not believe I can turn it around for your good? Can you not feel I love you? Why do you continue to accept less than you deserve? You don't understand My favor over your life. How can I show you I am ever present? When I called on Moses I gave him specific instructions. When I called on Abraham to sacrifice his son on the mountain, I placed a ram in the bush. I caused Paul, who had persecuted my followers, to change from his wick ways. You have to want to come out your drought by calling upon me and requesting what you need from me*".

Tired of feeling trap in a situation where there is no end to the madness? "Jesus said to him, 'I am the way, and the truth, and the life. No one come to the Father except through me'."-John 14:6. If you want to come full circle, you must lay down your drought and drink from the Cup of Life. Declare that you will become more connected to God in this season. Let the past stay where it is, without turning back to it. Declare yourself free.

Day 11

Time

Time gives us what we need before doing or saying anything. Time is a measure in which events can be ordered from the past through the present into the future. It takes time for a child to be developed in a mother's womb. It takes time for a child to grow from a baby to a toddler, to crawl then to walk. It takes time for a child to move from words on to sentences. It takes time to develop into a woman or man, and to experience love, to be a parent, or to heal from a hurtful wound. It takes time to develop a close relationship with God. It takes time to develop one's authentic writing and speaking voice. We must learn to wait.

Often, we can jump ahead and mess up a blessing God's sending our way. We are trying to design our fate, to orchestrate with whom we will spend our lives, when the Lord may have shown us someone different. We are trying to call ourselves into things the Lord never ordained. We are trying to promote ourselves when the Lord has said it is not so. We hurry and rush into decisions that come back to bite us, because we do not realize we serve an "On-Time" God who knows what's best for us.

This life we have here on earth is only temporary and we must handle it with care. If we do not, we will spend time off course, so God must re-route our specific time structure to put us back on track. Psalm 27:14 states, *"Wait on the Lord; be of good courage and he shall strengthen thine heart, wait I say on the Lord".* It takes time to do everything; we must learn to be still and wait before just doing it. Time will always reveal the truth!

Day 12

Not Yourself

Are you feeling weighed down with no relieve in sight? In Mark 5, as soon as Jesus came out of the boat He met a man *with* unclean spirits. The man dwelled among the tombs. He had often been bound with shackles and chains, but he had pulled the chains a part and broken the shackles into pieces. No one could contain him. The man walked night and day in the mountains and among the tombs, crying out and cutting himself with stones.

From afar, the man saw Jesus and ran to worship him. A spirit within him cried out with a loud voice, "*What have I to do with you, Jesus, Son of the highest God*? *I implore you by God that you do not torment me."* Jesus said, "*Come out of the man, unclean spirit*!" and Jesus asked the spirit, "What is your name*?* The unclean spirit answered*, "My name is Legion; for we are many."* Also, the spirits begged that Jesus would not send them out of the country. The demons begged Jesus to allow them to enter a herd of swine feeding nearby. Jesus gave them permission to enter the herd of swine; the herd jumped into the sea and drowned. Witnesses saw and ran to tell others. People came to Jesus talking with and the formerly demon-possessed man who was seated and clothed in his right mind. When Jesus prepared to leave, the man begged Jesus to go with Him. But Jesus replied "*No, go home to your friends, and tell them what great things the Lord has done for you, and how He has shown you compassion.*"

Many of us are not ourselves because of those we associate with. We believe all those around us are good for us, when many of them are not. We come to feel a certain way or develop attitudes, or even use language that does not reflect who we are by being around those who have different spirits. Those spirits can enter our spirits, so we find ourselves roaming night and day crying out from self- inflicted wounds. We become so weighed down that it can cause the loss of one's mind. Calling on Jesus, as the man in Mark 5, can release the shackles and chains of the unclean spirits within. We, too, can cry out, Matthew 12:43 states "*When an evil spirit leaves a person, it goes into the desert, seeking rest but finding none.*" We must be careful who we allow into our space; they may look genuine and innocent, but they may have come to destroy the destiny our Father laid for us.

Repeat these words every day: "*Submit yourself, therefore to God. Resist the devil, and he will flee from you.*" We should not give room to any spirit to dwell in us, except the Holy Spirit. Suit up in the full armor of God and seal any weak areas.

Day 13

A Lamp and a Light

Never dismiss a message God personally sent you? A young lady received instructions regarding this Scripture, "Your word is a lamp to my feet, and a light to my path."

A young lady was meeting someone and didn't know it was a divine assignment. As the young lady and another young lady were talking, God took center stage as the words pierced the lady's heart because she needed that encouragement.

She said to the young lady, "This strange thing happened with my phone. As I look at my phone this scripture constantly popped up "Your Word is a lamp to my feet and a light to my path". God dropped these words in the young lady's spirit: "*Go, home Dorothy*! *Just follow the yellow brick road. It will guide you all the way there. God has been telling you to come home to Him; His arms* are wide *open waiting on you*." The tears flowed from her eyes because she knew it was time.

Someone at this moment is truly broken, and struggling to build a life, but seem to keep being pushed back. Someone may be unhappy and displeased with the direction your life is going, but you don't know what to do. You have walked away from those who truly love you to follow what you perceived to be real, but turned into more hell to handle. You continue to seek man for understanding, although he cannot relieve your frustrations. You have dismissed every message God sent you to get out because you refused to believe.

God is saying "*Look my child! My word is the lamp to your feet and light to your path. So, walk down this yellow brick road and get that relief, get that joy, and get back your self-respect. Stop allowing idle thoughts to detour you from receiving the blessing I have for you. Take the first step and I'll take the next. Then watch how abundant your life will be.*"

Psalm 40:1-3 states "*I waited patiently for God to help me; then He listened and heard my cry. He lifted me out of the pit of despair, out from the bog and mire, and set my feet on a hard, firm path, and steadied me as I walked along. He has given me a new song to sing of praises to our God. Now many will hear of the glorious things He did for me, and stand in awe before the Lord, and put their trust in Him.*" Follow that light of life!

Day 14

Regroup

A mother was driving when her daughter asked, "*Mommy, do you understand about regrouping.*" The girl explained a problem in which 27 was to be taken away from 33. "See, *Mommy you must ask Big Daddy can you take one from the 3 over the 2, and make 3 over 7 into the number 13. The answer is 6.*" Her mother smiled and asked, "*Who taught you that explanation.*" The girl replied, "*My teacher.*"

The simplest lesson in life can help guide us in regrouping with Christ. It starts with our hearts. We use "*we think*" concepts to resolve our problems. We think our hearts are pure, but it can be consumed with hidden jealousy, ill feelings, or other things that shouldn't be there. We think our issues will disappear if we just tease God in prayer, to get what we want, but do not give our full heart. We think covering who we really are wouldn't matter to others, but it reveals our true motives. The "*we think*" concept takes God out of the equation of our problems. We must ask our "Big Daddy," God to assist us in taking away one issue at a time, to completely remove the filthiness from us.

"Therefore, get rid of all moral filth and the evil that is so prevalent and humbly accept the word planted in you, which can save you." James 1:21

We must put in the hard work on our jobs to receive dividends of our labor. Then the same is true in our spiritual development. Do a heart assessment, as well as, a whole regroup inventory. Review the results.

Day 15

Different

A young lady heard the gospel song "*Different*" came on the radio. The recording artist's recounting her testimony touched the young lady's heart and she started to replay her introduction to God. She, too, had never forgotten her roots in Him, but she did things outside of His will. The cycle continued until one day God called her name. That call made her to look at her life and how different she'd become.

God had placed a deep-rooted gift inside her until the time came for her to use it. He molded her to be beautifully made inside out. He gave her a genuine heart to love and share His word. He gave her a deep hunger for His Word where she ate it and interpreted it well. God watched how his master plan was being fulfilled in her life. She could only say, "*Thank you, Lord for making me different, singling* me *out for this season.*"

To be "*different*" in the Lord is to be "unusual." Being *different* in the Lord makes you love those who are against you. *Differen*t makes you dig deeper into

God's Word. Different can turn your life around for the better. *Different* triggers a desire inside of you to constantly have His name in your mouth to tell of His goodness. Being *different* causes that inner light of Christ to shine. Being *different* turns your prayer life into an intercession for all people. *Different* does much more; it does not cast out, but it causes one to stand out. 1 Peter 2:9 states "*But ye [are] a chosen generation, a royal priesthood, a holy nation, a peculiar people; that ye should shew forth the praises of Him who hath called you out of darkness into His marvelous light*". Embrace the *different* in you; you are unusual and peculiar. That's the way He made you.

Day 16

Heroes

Have you mistakenly called someone a "hero" when the facts didn't add up? What characteristics should a hero embody? In a movie released in 1992 movie called "*Hero,*" Dustin Hoffman portrayed a thief, and Geena Davis played a reported who was rescued from an airplane crash. The reporter couldn't see the man who saved her. His face was covered by the darkness, but she remembered his foul mouth, and that he'd left behind one of his shoes.

The reporter told everyone about her experience and wanted to find the "hero" who had saved everyone. After a brief search, they found a homeless man who had the match to the shoe left at the site of the crash. They turned his life around, but Hoffmann told the people that man they were showering accolades upon wasn't the one who'd actually rescued them. No one believed his story until the reporter discovered the truth. She thanked Hoffman for rescuing her and he replied, "*You're welcome.*"

Throughout history we have proclaimed and honored people as heroes. However, the ultimate hero, the one who deserves all credit and acknowledgement is Jesus. We should sing to Jesus the lyrics to a song made famous by Bette Midler: "*Did You ever know are our hero and everything we'd like to be? You are the One to make our cold and darkest moments so comforting, know You are so near. You are the one with all the glory. You are the beautiful face of peace to calm everything. You are the beautiful smile to hide the pain. We can fly higher than an eagle because You are the wind beneath our wings." It will never go unnoticed; we opened our hearts to You and You entered in.*" Lord God, You know everything. We know You are the greatest, the Hero of all heroes.

"For God sent not his Son into the world to condemn the world, but the world through him might be saved". John 3:17 Today, say thank you to our hero Jesus for all He has done.

Day 17

True Deliverance

Have you ever gone back to what God had delivered you from? 1 Kings, chapter 13, illustrates a powerful lesson on deliverance. There was a man of God traveled from Judah to Bethel by the word of the Lord, and Jeroboam stood by the altar to burn incense. The man of God cried out against the altar by the words of the Lord, and said, "*O altar, altar! Thus, says the Lord*: "'Behold, a child, Josiah by name, shall be born to the house of David; and on you he shall sacrifice the priests of the high places who burn incense on you, men's bones shall be burned on you.'" And the man of God gave a sign that same day saying, "'*This is the sign which the Lord has spoken: Surely the altar shall split apart, and the ashes on it shall be poured out*.'"

It did come to pass just as the man of God said and King Jeroboam heard what took place at the altar in Bethel. So, the king stretched out his hand towards the man of God, but his hand withered and he couldn't pull it back. The altar did just as the man of God said. And the King asked, "*Please entreat the favor of the*

Lord, your God, and pray for me, that my hand may be restored to me." The man of God entreated the Lord, and the king's hand was restored to him. The king asked the man of God to go home with him and refresh himself, and promised to give him a reward. The man of God said to the king, "*If you gave half of your house, I would not go with you nor would I eat bread nor drink water in this place. For it was commanded to me by the word of the Lord"* saying "*You shall not eat bread, nor drink water, nor return by the same way you came.*" And he departed in a different direction from the way he'd come to Bethel.

The man of God was only sent to do the Lord's work. The king couldn't see his evil ways and had the man of God arrested for speaking God's word at the altar. His hand withered because his action against the man of God. As he saw the word of God been fulfilled, he asked the man of God to ask his Lord to restore his hand. Then the king wanted him to go to his home, but the man of God declined because his assignment was completed and he obeyed the Lord's instructions by not returning the same way.

Too many times, we do not realize the significance of our deliverance. We have cried out to the Lord, "*O, Lord, O Lord, we need you to help us in our situation,*" as we brought our all to the altar. When the timing was right, He has spoken in a small voice what we should do, so that day by day we can start to walk toward our deliverance. Those who do not understand question our walk and talk against it, not knowing what they are trying to speak in our lives is also spoken in their own.

God unfolds everything in our deliverance, and we must truly worship Him with our all. We know we are not perfect, but we know the One who is. It is noticeable to those who say things they shouldn't; they want to know the God we are serving and ask for help. Their lives begin to change, and they want to show gratitude by asking us to join them, but we are instructed by our Lord that we cannot return the same way we came, and to go in a different direction. We should not return to things we left behind us; we cannot hang out, nor eat bread, nor drink water, once our Lord delivered us from a situation. "*For freedom Christ has set us free; stand firm therefore, and do not submit again to a yoke of slavery.*" Galatians 5:1 Truly embrace your deliverance because our Lord will show us what to do on our journey.

Day 18

A Little Black Book

In a comical film called "The Little Black Book" a young lady named Stacy Holt works as an associate producer on a daytime talk show. She believed she'd met the man of her dreams, but he is commitment-phobic. She discovered he carries a little black book and she was very curious to know what was inside of it.

She discussed the matter with a colleague, Barb, who convinced her to look inside. When Stacy looks inside his little black book, she sees a list of ex-girlfriends and sets up interviews with them to get closer to Derek, her boyfriend. Of course the plan backfired when she developed a friendship with one of his ex-girlfriends. Also, her colleague, Barb betrays her and exposes Derek as well as his ex-girlfriends on the talk show. Stacy was embarrassed and upset when everything unfolded on the show. When Stacy confronted Barb, her colleague dismissed her and told her the show was a masterpiece and that she had gotten what she wanted.

Enraged, Stacy wanted to harm Barb, but realized that if Barb could still look at herself after she'd destroy lives by airing that show, it was not worth it, so she walked away. Stacy was so intrigued with the little black book and thought she needed to know what was hidden. She caused a great deal of grief in Derek's life, his ex-girlfriends' lives, and in her own life because of her curiosity…she had to know.

Many times, we are carrying our little black books around and not knowing it's so obvious for others to see. They want to get close or find a common ground to crack open our little black books. It's like they want to know what makes us the way we are. They want to discover our weak points to use them against us. When we allow them in, they take note of all they find out about us from our little black books. When they believed an opportunity has come to expose us, it becomes a testimony of our faith.

We are aware of the contents of our little black books and have gone into prayer about what has been written in them. Jeremiah 29:11 states, "For I know the plans I have for you, declares the Lord, plans to prosper and not to harm you, plans to give you hope and a future."

Our Lord and Savior designed the course of how our book of life is written. Whether or not we are aware of others' motives to snoop in our little black books, we must keep our eyes on God. He knows the reasoning behind the snoop and He has written it down as well. Be watchful and prayerful always.

Day 19

Baggage

A young lady felt very blessed by the news of a dear friend's receiving her breakthrough. That joy reminded her of Erykah Badu's 2000 classic song "*Bag Lady*." In the lyrics, a bag lady is a woman who is not able to commit to a new relationship because her emotional baggage overtakes her, makes her wary, and afraid to get close to people.

The song lyrics tell the bag lady to pack light, and to have hope for the future. She has to learn to release every bag she's carrying--- whether it's a Gucci bag, a grocery bag, a plain paper sack, or even a nickel bag--- because it's crowding her space. "*Let it go! Let it go*!" To be free, the bag lady has to let the baggage go!

Excessive baggage wears you down. Break the cycle of carrying emotional baggage. Instead, begin a new relationship with Christ. Strive to live according to His Word. Put down your pity bag. Stop feeling sorry for yourself and carrying the pity bag so everyone knows it and feels sorry for you too. Drop the misery bag, because when things are not going right for you, it makes everyone around you miserable too. Lay down that low self-esteem bag. You are a child of the Most High God, made in His image! Let go of the jealousy bag as well. Don't hold a grudge or turn up your nose at someone else's success or the way he/she carries himself. (You don't really know their story.) Let go of that emotional bag that keeps you glued to the hurt someone caused you. Even the unstable bag should be left behind; it takes your peace of mind and keeps you moving from one place to the next without roots to ground you.

The list can go on of the different types of baggage you could carry. God will not enter a defiled temple, so put down all of the baggage weighing you down. He's watching; He knows about the many bags you are carrying; He wants you to open your mouth daily to give them to Him.

Hebrews 12:1-2 states *"Therefore we also, since we were surrounded by so great a cloud of witness. Let us lay aside every weight, and the sin which so easily ensnares us, and let us run with endurance the race that set before us, looking unto Jesus, the Author and Finisher of our faith, who for the joy that was set before Him endured the cross, despising the shame, had sat down at the right hand of the throne of God."* Give up your many baggage. God will carry you.

Day 20

A Secret Place

As a mother she watched the kids playing a game of Hide and Seek, her mind flashed back to the time she'd played the game as a child. She remembered: one person turned his back and counted to 20 while leaning against a tree or post that served as home base, while the other children scattered; they ran around to try to find a secret place to hide. When the person stopped counting, he or she shouted, "*Ready or not, here I come!*" Then, the person who'd counted ran around trying to find all the children. If the counter found someone, he or she had to take the place as the seeker.

The children would burst out of their secret places running toward the base to be safe. The mother remembered how they'd ran and she remembered their laughter, as they played this game. She recalled how the children peeped to see if there were a clear path to get to the tree, while others who had already made it back to the tree safely, waited to play the game again. Finally someone would be chosen to be the counter for the new round. The mother smiled as she remembered how much fun it used to be playing the game.

We are often like children playing a game of Hide and Seek, when we enter our secret place. There are not people running around as we kneel at the altar to talk with the Father about what's bothering us. We get comfortable there, then block out the distractions of our minds, our hearts, and our souls. We wait for a clear path to go into that safe, secret place. We do not peek our heads up; instead we bow them, and with closed eyes, feel the Spirit of the Living God surround us.

Ask the Lord: *"What can I do, when I have done all I can? What can I say, when I have said all I could say?"* And the Lord, (The Counter) will reply, "*My child, you are doing it* right now, as you are *getting in your secret place, your place to worship. I can meet your needs as they are brought to My feet at this altar.*" Then, suddenly, your secret place will be filled with much praise and worship as you consider how good He has been.

There is none like our Lord, none who can do the things He has done for us. When we enter our secret place, we are protected in His arms. For Psalm 119:114 says, "*You are my hiding place and my shield; I hope in Your Word.*"

Day 21

An Undercover Agent

In a 1992 film called *Deep Cover* a police officer named Russell Stevens is recruited by DEA to go undercover in a major sting operation in Los Angeles. Stevens' purpose was to pretend he was a big-time drug dealer to find evidence to bring down the king pin. Stevens posed as a drug dealer, John Hull, to infiltrate the drug ring and he worked his way up in the network of the West Coast's largest drug importer.

To continue to keep his true identity secret, he moved into a cheap hotel and began to deal drugs. He lived the life of a drug dealer. He witnessed the corruption within the drug operation and learned there were corrupt police officers involved in this assigned sting operation. When the DEA moved in, Stevens had gathered enough proof to testify in court. He had to be removed from the case before things went too far.

Stevens had only gone deep undercover to exposed truth the drug crimes, but he got caught up with the John Hull identity. He had to blow open the case before the DEA Special Unit tried to pin everything on him. As the truth was revealed, Stevens left the DEA lawyer standing in amazement.

Often, we really don't look at the purpose, the reasons we are connected to certain places, people, or situations. We are not *just there* to be too involved, but each one of us has an assigned purpose to learn all we must learn and move to the next assignment. We are recruited by a DEA Special Agent (God) to carry out an assignment to discover truth.

He allows us to get close/with certain people, places, or situations to give us the experiences so when the day comes to tell the truth, we will have the proof. Yes, we will be connected to some individuals to whom we will stay connected to for a life time, but there will be many who will fall off. We must listen and follow the instruction of our DEA Special Agent (God) who gives us the specifics, and we shouldn't go so deep undercover that we lose focus on its true purpose. We have only been placed to expose the truth with boldness.

II Timothy 2:15 reminds us to: "*Study to shew thyself approved unto God, a workman that needeth not be ashamed, rightly dividing the word of truth,"* Stand on truth as you move from one assignment to the next. We are not to linger too long on an assignment, but to study to gain strength.

Day 22

Friendship

A young man who'd been fighting for his friend, Jesus, found himself in a difficult situation, one that went against his beliefs. He struggled with what had taken place as everyone told him not to do it. He was led to stand up for God.

He'd gone into the sanctuary to ask God for guidance when the pastor entered the room and asked him if he needed help with anything. He told the pastor about his dilemma and the pastor gave him certain passages of scriptures to read. The young man gave the pastor a strange look as if to ask if that was it. The pastor saw his skepticism and reiterated that he would find the answer in those scriptures.

After reading and studying, the young man mounted the podium and stood up for God. He'd studied and presented before his peers on the knowledge of God's existence. He faced much opposition from his professor. When he was asked why he was doing what he was doing, his response was: *"Jesus is my friend and it is my place to take a stand on His behalf because He did it for me."* He left the person pondering on his words about Jesus' being his friend.

The word, "friend" has been used so loosely that we don't understand its true meaning. We associate with individuals we believe we have something in common, but having things is common with someone does not constitute true friendship. Be careful of who you call your friend.

A friend is someone who will kneel at the altar with us and help to bear what troubles us. A friend listens, before speaking. A friend will lift your spirit when you're discouraged. A friend is faithful and committed. A friend celebrates your growth in Christ and will not ask you to choose him/her over Him. A friend always brings peace, and not mess. A friend loves unconditional, and through it all.

Who wouldn't want a friend like Him? He has sent individuals in our lives to help us on this journey. They are our assigned angels, our brothers and sisters in Christ. Jesus, the Christ is the only friend we need. Proverbs 11:14 states, *"Where there is no guidance, a people fall, but in an abundance of counselors there is safety."*

Day 23

Suffering

As a lady stood under the shade waiting for her food, she noticed a young man who was flushed and sweating from the heat on his skin. She could see his frustration and noticed his hesitancy to ask for help, but he did finally ask for money for gas.

An older gentleman told the young man to pull around to the pump, so he could get some gas. Before the lady drove off and she began to talk with Jesus to ask Him to help His children in their season of suffering.

He reminded her of David's suffering. King David plotted to kill an innocent man to cover up his secret. When the report came back to him that it was done, David took the man's wife and made her his. The Lord sent Nathan to confront David and to reveal that the Lord's sent out a punishment for what he had done. He explained to David that his son with Bathsheba would die. When the child was sick, David fasted and asked the Lord not to take him. He sat on the ground without food or drink pleading with the

Lord. However, the child suffered because of David's selfish act and he knew it as well.

The lady realized that one might never know the cause of an individual's suffering. All she could do was pray for those going through a season of suffering.

Many times, we do not look at the cause of our season of suffering. We are quick to say, *"I didn't do anything to deserve this."* We must look at our behavior and ask ourselves what part we played; and be truly being honest with ourselves. Entertaining a corrupted conversation, we shouldn't be involved with, or playing both sides to get along, comes back to bite us.

We never think what might bring us to a period of suffering. It could be just our time to suffer because of God's plan for us. We must understand our season of suffering is not by accident but by design. James 1:2-4 reminds us to, "*Count it all joy, my brothers, when you meet trials of various kinds, for you know the testing of your faith produces steadfastness. And let steadfastness have its full effect, that you may be perfect and complete, lacking in nothing."*

Suffering does not feel good, but we must keep a praying, praising, and worshiping through it all. Our deliverance comes through our continuous talks with our Lord and Savior. Our suffering will not last always.

Day 24

Golden Child

The 1986 film *The Golden Child* illustrates spiritual warfare between good and evil. In the movie a young boy, a golden child, has mystical abilities. The golden child lives with monks in a secure location, where he demonstrates his power to revive the dead. During the monks' communion with the boy, a band of villains led by a mysterious man, Sardo Numspa, invades the monastery, slaughters the monks, and then, abducts the boy.

In the meantime, Kee Nang watches a TV show to see a social worker named Chandler Jarrell talk about his latest case of a missing girl named Cheryl Mosley. Nang seeks out Jarrell the next day and informs him of the kidnapping of the golden child and that he's been chosen to save the child. Chandler, however, doesn't take Kee seriously; he walked away. Soon after, Cheryl Mosley is found dead from blood loss in an abandoned house smeared with Tibetan graffiti on the walls and a pot of blood-soaked oatmeal. Chandler learned the house had been the holding place for the child and Kee introduced him to a mystic expert doctor, Kala, who explained what was going on.

The three tracked down the motorcycle gang Cheryl had been a part of which led to some clues about the case. Because Numspa suspected Tong was a traitor, he killed him. Chandler still didn't take the case seriously until Numspa appeared in his dream and showed the Ajanti Dagger he needed, and he received a burn on his arm. Then, Chandler and Kee travel Tibet because he'd finally decided to help find the missing child.

Upon arrival in Tibet, Chandler was introduced to the high priest who was Kee's father. Chandler had to pass an obstacle course to get the dagger, and he did it. They returned to the States where they needed to pass customs with the dagger. When they failed, Numspa tried to intervene but was not successful. Chandler began to see the spiritual forces beyond human flesh; Numspa turned out to be a demon from hell who wanted to kill the golden child.

Chandler faced many challenges to save the child. He felt the boy's power and he witnessed the boy's power. He used the dagger to stab Numspa through his heart. When Chandler experienced the power from both good and evil. His whole outlook changed.

Many of us are like Chandler, not really looking at the significance of finding The Golden Child. We have heard the greatness of *The Golden Child, Jesus, the Christ,* chosen by Our Father to fulfill a mission for all of us. Although we have read about it, and have even seen videos about it, like Chandler in the film, we don't quite connect the dots. We have experienced something only Jesus could do for us. He walked among mankind, felt our struggles, and faced spiritual battles as well. Not once did He take His eyes off what He set out to do. He knew the main source of the power within Him and committed Himself to stay focused.

Christ faced a Numspa-like evil one who threw all kinds of temptations and distractions at Him, but Christ relied on God's power. Revelation 17:14 says, "*These will wage war against the Lamb, and the Lamb will overcome them, because he is Lord of Lords and King of Kings, and those who are with Him are the called and chosen and faithful*".

We must join in the search for the true *The Golden Child* to receive the deliverance, the truth, and the purpose to which we are called.

Day 25

Take it Back

Although Job had wealth, good health, children, and was very faithful to God, Satan approached God to challenge Job's integrity and suggested that Job served God simply because He protected him.

God, confident of Job faithfulness, allowed Satan to attack him: however, God would not allow Satan to touch Job's soul. Satan mounted a fierce assault on God's son; he stripped Job of his wealth, health, and children. In spite of the assaults, Job didn't curse God, even when he could not explain why he was going through what seemed unending suffering. He kept his faith planted in God, even as his friends assumed he had done something wrong. Even his wife tried to convince him to stop praising the Lord. Job stood on the declaration, "*The Lord will take care of it all.*" Job's suffering taught him patience and to accept the will of God. God restored Job double for his faithfulness.

Sometimes we really don't understand the reason for our suffering, because it may not be based on anything we have done. God allows the suffering to occur, so that we can become stronger in our faith. The enemy watches for the little cracks to gain entry into your life, to try to take you back to the fallen state he'd had you in before. He can't stand the fact he lost you! He will try to invade your relationship with your spouse, your children, your workplace, your siblings, and even your parents, to rattle your nerves. The enemy sits back, smiling as he plots, and witnesses his tactics working in your life.

You must declare: *"I am no longer intimidated by Satan's attacks. I cannot do anything to change what took place, but God will guide me to be better in this current race I am running."*

Pray about the things that haunt you and God will give you the victory over them. The uncontrollable tears will cease, along with the feelings of worthlessness. Prayer will remove your doubts, because you will declare with confidence: "*My Father's got me*." Declare: *"I will not allow the deceiver the satisfaction that he gets to me. I am taking back my joy, my peace, and my happiness because greater is He that is in me."*

Remember: *"Many are the affliction of the righteous; but the Lord delivered him out of them all."*

Psalm 34:19 Stand on God's word and continue to take back what's yours.

Day 26

Healing

In deep mediation these words came to mind: "*God wants to heal you everywhere you hurt. He will see you through He will take your pain away. He will provide for you every day. Just lift your hands and say, "'Lord, I need you right away.'* "

Instantly, Luke 8:40-47 about the woman with the issue of blood fell into the lady's spirit; the passage illustrated the power of Jesus' healing. When Jesus returned the multitude welcomed Him, for they were all waiting for Him. Jairus, the ruler of the synagogue, fell at Jesus' feet and begged Him to come to his house because his only daughter, who was about twelve years old, was dying. Jesus was traveling with Jairus to his home through the crowd, when a woman who'd had flowing blood for twelve years, came behind Jesus and touched the border of his garment. Immediately her flow of blood stopped.

Jesus asked, "Who touched Me?" Despite the crowd of people, around Him, Jesus said, "*Somebody touched me, for I perceived power going out from me.*"

Then the woman came forth from hiding, trembling as she fell before Him. The woman declared to Him in the presence of all the people, the reason she had touched Him and how she had been healed immediately.

Jesus, said to the woman, "*Daughter, be of good cheer; your faith had made you well. Go in peace.*" Jesus was still speaking when someone came up to tell Him Jarius' daughter had died. And he turned to leave for his next assignment.

Many of us are experiencing an uncontrollably flow for many years in our lives. We have seen and spoken with our physician about our problems, but nothing seems to work. In our deep meditation time, we have sought after God, and listened carefully for answers to our condition. Take comfort in these words: *"God wants to heal us everywhere we hurt. He will see you through, and He will take our pain away. He will provide for us every day.*"

We must lift our hands and saying, "*Lord, we need you right away.*" Our faith in Him will cause our uncontrollably flow to stop because we've touched the hem of His garment as we called out to Him. Jesus feels the power moving through Him and knows who has touched Him. He has seen our struggles, our disappointments, and our sadness during our uncontrollably flow.

III John 1:2 states, *"Beloved, I wish above all things that thou mayest prosper and be in health, even thy soul prospereth."* Our Father does not want us to remain in our present condition. He's waiting on us to give it all to Him, so we can be prosperous in every way. Don't speak death in your life. God wants to heal us everywhere we hurt; just open our mouths to Him.

Day 27

Praise Break

The blessings of God flow like a domino effect. A young lady reflected on how prayer helped her to push forward, despite what was going on in her life. She was introduced to the most powerful technique to overcome, to endure, and to be a living witness of God's goodness because of a mighty vessel.

That mighty vessel saw a broken spirit that needed to live and not die. The young lady offered her prayer to mend her broken spirit, which changed her life. She didn't know what was inside until she started speaking to God and she stopped running when there was an altar call during the service; she learned to have altar calls all the time.

Prayer pushed her through the pain, through the tears, through the low moments, and through her condemnation of herself; it pushed her to be what her Father called her to be. Her focus shifted to offering to men or women what was given to her, so all the binding chains could fall away and instead become linked in unity to serve their Father together.

She was so blessed, so full, so happy, and so thankful for that push; she was blessed to see others transformed into their divine purpose. It was enough for her to praise Him with everything she had.

True worshipers give our Father everything. Did you know your struggles could be used to bring in the lost? Did you realize you had all that you had? Start talking to God. Feel and see the power of God moving in you. It bubbles up on the inside, and stirs up, so that you can't help, but to tell it all.

You've opened your heart for change, so God could perform open heart surgery to remove all the pain, the bitterness, the confusion, and the brokenness. He's filled it with unconditional love, the love that drew you to Him. His transforming love will do the same for those you touch. Your struggles pushed you to strive for more of Him. Every chance you get, thank the Lord for pushing you through it all. His push saved your life.

Day 28

A Life Coach

A young lady received a flyer about how to reach one's full potential. For a fee, the flyer claimed it could help people who were striving for excellence. The young lady kept debating whether she should go. At the last minute, she signed up to attend the workshop which was being held on a Saturday she was free.

She was impressed by what she learned in the session and wanted to know more. Although there were additional fees to continue the program, she decided she would continue it. However, God blocked it instantly. God showed her she didn't need to pay for a life coach because she had one already. He knew the hunger and thirst she possessed because she had grasped every opportunity He'd given her. He spoke these words into her spirit: "*Did you hear me say anything about getting a life coach*? *Have I ever asked you for a fee to gain knowledge that is completely free? Don't fall for the trap of the enemy to strip away your gifts and* then *leave you alone and broken. I cleansed you from every impurity and molded you, to live in your true purpose. Just keep listening to My voice only; pay attention to My guidance for directions to move forward."*

The young lady quickly withdrew from the program to attend God's life coaching seminar. She needed more one-on-one time with the Heavenly Father for her growth and expansion.

We are quick to do things on our own, thinking we are *helping* God, but our "helping" delays our future. We make what seems to be rational decisions, then are not pleased with the results. We search for things or people to make us whole, unwilling to wait on God's promise. We continue to search for answers, but cannot find anything or anyone greater than God.

Stop trying to hurry the progress or process. Our mission is to be good stewards and listen to our Father's instructions. He is the only Life Coach, Counselor, Healer, Doctor, and Father who can do all things.

We must understand that we must take everything to God in prayer and then, wait on Him. Matthew 6:33 states, "*But seek ye first the kingdom of God and his righteousness, and all these things shall be added to you.*"

Day 29

The Key

Hearing the testimony of a sister's walk with Christ was inspirational:

"The day I met you I knew I had to seek employment to take care of the bills I had amassed. I really didn't know it was fate that ordained my walk with my Father. I was consumed by worry, until, God placed a situation in my life to get my full attention. When I walked in your office. I didn't know God was setting me up for the biggest miracle in my life. I was truly broken and trying to hide my pain, but you saw it and went beyond your job description to give me what I needed, and I am forever grateful.

That day when I left your office, I became employed with the Lord and very eager to know more of Him. Now, I know my purpose because you pointed me toward it. It was given from our Father. Because of your help, I broke free from my caged mindset and saw the bigger picture. I can feel the linked chain effect because I gave back to someone who needed what I needed several months ago. It made me feel good to assist her in breaking her caged mindset."

The young lady could feel the overflow pouring out as she responded to her beautiful words.

Too often, we are controlled by our inner thoughts and we don't truly listen to our hearts. We must understand this gives the enemy space to sneak in and take over. We must discern whether it is God speaking to us or the enemy. We can be too caught up in our emotions or around so much negativity that we want to give up. We fall to pieces over our health and take ownership of a diagnosis. We can become too comfortable with our wrongdoing and make excuses to justify it.

God tells us to consider the errors of our ways. The Word tells us not to conform to this world, but to be transformed by the renewal of our minds to break that prison state of mind and move outside of the box.

God wants us to stop feeding into the seed of Satan. Psalm 2:3 states, "*Let us break their chains, they cry, and free ourselves from slavery to God.*" Use the key to be released from the caged mentality to receive a spirit mind.

The Number 7

One night, a young lady was sleeping when the story of Joseph entered her dreams. As she tossed and turned in her sleep, she asked the Lord to speak to her about her situation. She was directed to open her Bible and turned to Genesis 41.

Pharaoh had a strange dream and couldn't understand the meaning. He asked for an interpretation of his dream, but no one could explain it. His chief butler remembered a young man he'd met in prison named Joseph who had interpreted his dream and told Pharaoh about him. Pharaoh called for Joseph to explain the strange dream he'd had for two nights. Joseph told Pharaoh he would have seven years of wealth and seven years of famine. Joseph also explained to Pharaoh that he needed to prepare to store up food during his bountiful years for the seven years of famine that would follow.

After reading the chapter, the young lady went into full worship because she knew God was going to turn around her struggle. She began to thank Him for giving her a humble attitude, for His teaching her how to wait on her turn, for chastising her when she needed it, and for continuously purging her for this season. It wasn't easy, but she kept calling for His help. She understood the number 7 meant, "completion," and her completion would take place in due season.

We have each gone through difficult storms and yearned to see the light after a dark and stormy ride. The good news is Jesus will walk with you through the storm of the living from pay check to pay check, the storm of denied promotions, the storm of feeling on the verge of a nervous wreck, or the storm of living in a hellish home without peace.

Jesus will hold you through any storm because His love is true. He can stop the cries of your heart. God will throw you a life jacket to grab hold to in a storm's strong waves so that you will not sink. During your years of famine, have faith; know your years of wealth will be pouring in.

"*Wait on the Lord: be of good courage, and he shall strengthen thine heart; wait, I say on the Lord.*" Psalm 27:14

Day 31

Increase

During the service, a young woman listened as Donald Lawrence's musical rendition of Jabez's prayer was being sang:

"*Bless me, bless me. O Lord, bless me indeed. Enlarge my territory. Oh God, bless me, indeed. God, I pray that You would bless me. Increase. Increase; I pray for increase. Enlarge my territory. O God, bless me indeed. I stand, and I pray that You would bless me.*" Within a few minutes of the altar call, the congregation was looking towards heaven requesting to be blessed from their Father in every way.

The young lady reflected on Matthew 14:19, "*Then He commanded the multitude to sit down on the grass. And He took the five loaves of bread and the two fish, and looking up to heaven, He blessed and broke and gave the loaves to the disciples; and the disciples gave to the multitude.*"

Ask the Lord to bless you in every way. Ask Him to deliver you from the past, from what has occurred in your life. Ask God to encourage you that you might lift yourself up, instead of putting yourself down. God demonstrates in Matthew 14:19 what He can do with a little, and He fed a multitude.

Pray Jabez's prayer over yourself: "*Bless me. Bless me, O Lord! Increase, Increase, I pray for increase, so you can enlarge my territory.*" Be released from the brokenness. Nothing is impossible for God. He can use you and give you instructions to tell everyone about Him. You can feed a multitude with what God has given you. You will receive your increase; it shall be increased with a purpose.

Isaiah 65:24 says, "*And it shall come to pass, that before they call, I will answer; and while they are yet speaking, I will hear.*" Do not doubt the power of God. He's maximizing your life in every way! You can feel it.

Day 32

Peace in the Midst of it

Three ladies from different walks of life, were linked because of their common love for the Lord. The Lord allowed an opportunity for the three to discuss, to rejoice, to testify, and to dance about the goodness of God in a parking lot. It didn't matter who was watching, walking or even driving by, because they were on fire for God.

Before the fellowship end, one of the ladies prayed a powerful prayer. As she spoke, the area became so quiet and still that the wind blew into the circle of prayer. The Lord swept through, because his children were giving Him glory for what he had done and was about to do in their lives. When they said "Amen" in unison, they stepped back, and the sound of cars, people, and laughter started again. The women shouted "My Lord!" in exaltation, for they had not experienced anything like this before.

Like these women, we do not understand the full power of prayer. We must not think on what to say in prayer, but allow the Holy Spirit to direct our hearts on what needs to be said on behalf of others. We must step aside, so God takes center stage to touch His children in their time of need.

Prayer is our 9-1-1 to the Father, the Son, and the Holy *Spirit* to intervene on our issues. The saying, "*When we begin to call on the name of Jesus something starts to happen,*" means prayer enables our salvation, deliverance, and sanctification by feeling Him in the spirit.

Acts 4:12 states, *"There is no other name under heaven given among men by which we must be saved."* Do not underestimate the power of prayer. Trust and believe it still works.

Day 33

Building a Relationship

Sometimes it is difficult to bond with your child. A single mother took for granted her relationship with her daughter. The terms of a bitter, nasty divorce, from her ex-husband cut into her fabulous lifestyle. She could no longer keep the staff she'd had when they were married. More than that, it distanced her from her daughter because her daughter had lost the one person who kept her straight.

Their relationship fell into pieces because the mother had focused so much time catering to her husband, that she neglected her responsibilities as a mother. Her children were strangers to her. The strain weighed heavily on her; she asked her daughter if she loved her. Her daughter replied, "*Momma, I love you, but I don't know you.*" After this response, the mother extended her hand to introduce herself to her daughter who did the same. They hugged as they began to forge a new relationship.

As parents we may come to question our children's actions towards us. We may dissect the issues, without being able to discern the root of the problem. We sometimes allow negative thoughts to overtake our minds, so we fail to notice what we are putting out to our children; they may see you do things they don't like it. We must be mindful of speaking to them in a harsh tone, and be careful that we carve out time to spend with them. Be mindful of the fact that they are little people too, who want your love and respect, just as they give it to you.

Isaiah 54:13 states "*All your children shall be taught by the Lord, and great shall be the peace of your children*" Stop being frustrated with your children; instead, celebrate the precious gift of having them. Build a relationship with them.

Day 34

Secrets

In Medea's *Family Reunion*, two sisters had a close relationship and always confided in each other. Their mother, however, gave more attention to the younger daughter because she had a different father than her older daughter.

One night they were at their grandmother's house talking, enjoying one another, until their mother showed up and demanded the younger daughter to leave. The older daughter asked their mother why she hate her so much, but her mother would not respond. The older sister said, *"I remember when you allowed your husband to have his way with me and never said a word as you dressed me up to prepare me for him."*

The mother confessed, "*My mother did the same thing to me and I learned to cope with it. My husband was going to leave me, but he wanted you and I had to do what I needed to do to keep what I wanted.*"

The younger daughter was shocked that her father had done those things to her sister. She couldn't believe her mother would allow such a thing. The older daughter pleaded for her mother's love, but she turned away from her, and waited downstairs for the younger daughter to leave with her.

Secrets can cause deep wounds that affect your growth in Christ. You may try to get the one who caused the pain to apologize or you may try to create a façade, so that no one will ever see your true pain, or you may seek attention from your mother or father who neglected you, or you may become confused about what love is or what it feels like to have love in your life.

God shows us, His children, that we are not what has been done to us; we can rise above it. We should not beat up ourselves with "*what ifs*." Although what took place may have been awful, you have the power to turn it into a positive ministry to save others. God will get the glory from your commitment to be transparent. There is a King living inside; let Him reign.

Forgive! Forgive! Let it go so you can be set free. You are not a fatherless or motherless child. You have *Someone* who can give you much more, our Lord and Savior, the Father of all.

The Fight of Your Life

I Samuel 18-21 illustrates the rise and fall of the relationship between Saul and David. At first Saul showed David much love and honor. Whatever Saul asked of him, David did without hesitation. David won many victories as he served as commander over the men he was assigned.

From the day, Saul heard a song of victory, in which the men shouted out his name, but celebrated David's name even more, a rage of fury stirred in Saul's spirit, so King Saul eyed David in jealously.

David didn't change; he continued to be loyal to Saul. However, something rose within Saul that he couldn't shake off. The more Saul asked David to do; the more King Saul saw the younger man's successes as the Lord's being with him. It came to the point that Saul wanted David dead. Although Saul planned and schemed to have David killed; all of his plans backfired.

David was confused by Saul's behavior and questioned what he'd done to his king to make him plot his destruction. David's only choice was to stay out of Saul's path, and to fight for his life. While David hid himself to elude those who would have assassinated him, he vowed to continue to show love towards Saul. Through it all, David listen carefully to the Lord's instructions and did not retaliate against the king; he left Saul in the Lord's hands.

Many of us have felt as if we were in the fight of a life time, because we, too, have had an experience similar to David's. We too have been close to someone and have opened our arms to show love. We, too, have acted on behalf of the person without any hesitation. Then, there is an action by the person that takes you by surprise, so that you question what you've done to prompt it.

Your tactics are to stay in your lane, to remove yourself from the situation, and to vow before God to treat that person the same, no what matter he or she has done.

Romans 12:19 states "*Dearly beloved, avenge not yourself, but [rather] give place upon wrath: for it is written, vengeance [is] mine; saith the Lord.*" The most powerful weapon in your arsenal is the war room of prayer where you can tell the Lord about it. It is not a physical fight, but a spiritual one in which only God can guide you through.

Day 36

My Sister's or Brother's Keeper

Katie, a young girl dying of acute leukemia touched her sister and brother during her illness. She had been diagnosed in her childhood, and the disease caused her to undergo many changes. Watching her in the struggle with the cancer, affected everyone, especially her sister Anna, who was labeled as a savior child who was born to help her sister.

Their brother observed the relationship between his sisters. Katie knew the leukemia was taking a toll on her body; she knew as well it was dividing her family. She told Anna not to give up her kidney. Katie explained to their parents Anna was important too. It caused their mother to go into a rage because of Anna's refusal to help. Katie sued her parents to be emancipated, to gain the right to make her own medical decision.

Their brother couldn't stay by in silence, while he witnessed his family's crumbling; he told them Katie had instructed Anna to refuse to donate her organ. The mother was shocked by the news of Katie's wish to die peacefully without any more surgery. The dying daughter held her mother in her arms as she slipped away in peace.

Often, we can misinterpret what the word, *"keeper"* means. We are to comfort in a time of need. We are to show love, not hatred, envy, or jealousy towards one another. We are to listen, and not be hypocritical. We are supposed to be supportive, not keep a tally of who did what. We are supposed to encourage one another, not destroy others with our tongues. We are supposed to be honest.

We must know that God created us to help one another, not try to control them. Malachi 2:10 states, *"Have we not all one Father? Has not one God created us? Why do we deal treacherously with one another; by profaning the covenant of the fathers?"* We were created to be our sister's or brother's keeper.

Day 37

A Miracle

In a conversation with her cousin, a young lady related how she identified herself with several stories in the Bible:

She explained, *"I understood the issue Hagar encountered with Sara. When I couldn't forgive myself, I was just like David who sat down and grieved over the loss of his baby. Then, I had an experience like Ruth when Naomi showed Ruth where she needed to go... Finally, God checked me just like he did Paul, during his experience on the road to Damascus. I can truly see the miracle God had worked in me to allow me to visualize myself in this great book."*

Her cousin, amazed by what she'd said, replied, *"I'm going back and read to identify who I am like!"*

Sometimes we don't see the miracle God has wrought in us. We can see in others but not ourselves. If we can see a change in our attitude, that's God humbling us. If we can see a difference in our thinking process, that's God giving us wisdom and understanding. If we can see that we don't respond the way we used to, that's God maturing us. If we can see growth in our spiritual walk, that's God molding us. We must acknowledge God in all things he has done for us; acknowledge the miracle God has work out of us; and share the good news with others.

"But may the God of all grace, who called us to His eternal glory by Christ Jesus, after you have suffered a while, perfect, establish, strengthen, and settle you." 1 Peter 5:10

Day 38

Release It

A young lady gave her shoulder for a friend to cry on who had a dilemma and came to her for help. They talked as the friend hugged and began to sob:

The young lady consoled her saying, "*You are going to be all right. You are just going through a molding process that you don't understand, but God's got something in store for you. Don't give up. Don't allow this to break you; it will make you strong. Don't worry about this, because in God you have a true friend who will be there anytime. You must pray constantly and get to know Him for yourself. I'll pray along with you, but He wants you to surrender your all to Him. All is well." The young lady repeated, "All is well."*

Although you may be dealing with a broken heart, there is someone to understand your outcry. God wants you to come to Him. Do not continue to walked around with the burdens you have carried, you need a release and to feel better. Whatever the burden--- *loss of a job, inability to reach a compromise, attacks at every turn, or the loss of loved ones*--- don't worry and don't wonder how much more you will have to bear. God gave you a Comforter, the "Holy Spirit" to guide you during your troubling times. He wants you to come to Him first, so His words of wisdom may speak to your heart.

Stop walking around with a big "S" on your chest; you are not superman or superwoman. You can't do it all alone. Release it. You will need a shoulder to cry on, God will instruct and send an appointed person …someone who will give you what you need in your time of despair.

Day 39

Gather Your Blessing

A man standing at his post, looked out in his field and saw a young lady he'd never seen before. When he asked who she was, his workers told him that the young lady had come back with Naomi. He asked his workers to tell her to come to see him.

As the young lady was walking towards the man, he introduced himself, and told her he admired what she was doing for Naomi. He invited her to sit down to break bread with him. She ate and drank as she conversed with the man, and put some food away for Naomi. She thanked him for his kindness and asked if she might be excused to return to her work.

When Ruth returned to the fields, the landowner instructed his workers to lay down bundles of grain, so she could pick them up easily. After a hard day of work, the young lady took what she had gathered and the food to Naomi who was pleased with her efforts and asked where she worked. The young lady recounted her whole day to Naomi.

Naomi said, "*Oh, that's Boaz. He's family and began to describe his character to Ruth.*" Naomi knew the blessing behind Ruth's gathering and advised her on what to do to show her gratitude towards him. Ruth didn't know what was going to take place as she worked in the field and she didn't know she was working in the fields of a gentle man who had a soft heart, who had laid down blessings for her to gather. It was only God who had set her up to be blessed in such a manner, and she accepted it; she received it without any hesitation.

Often, we do not know what we are walking into until it happens. We are doing what we must do to make it each day. We do not realize that someone may be looking at us and asking who we are. We are so focus on getting the job done that we don't take notice, until the day someone asks us to sit down and break bread. After eating and conversing, we might go back to finish our work day, believing it's the end. Blessings can be poured in our paths and as we see them being laid down, we should pick them up, as we come upon them. Ezekiel 34:26 states, *"And I will make them and the places round about my hill a blessing; and I will cause the shower to come down in his season; there shall be showers of blessing."* God knows what we need as we gather the blessings in our paths because it's our season to receive them. Enjoy our Father's love.

Day 40

Rattlesnakes

A powerful and though-provoking author and lecturer told a story about rattlesnakes; it is a modern day parable:

"I was in the house when my husband came into the room and asked if I knew there was a rattlesnake in the backyard. He said he'd stepped on something unusual while walking out back; it was the head of a rattlesnake. The snake made a loud rattling, ringing, sound, and slithered across the backyard. My husband told me he moved quickly before it could bite him. I was shocked and hurriedly called the fire department to handle the matter."

Have you allowed rattlesnakes to enter your backyard, fearful of what they might do? Are you failing to see how they tell on themselves as they approach? Say "*No,*" to cut them off, and call on Jesus to decapitate these rattlesnakes to regain your comfort and peace. Don't allow the snakes' loud sound to shake the very foundation we stand on.

We have been so accustomed to the rattlesnake's venom that it stagnates our confidence, preventing us from pressing forward. The snakes deceive us into believing we are trapped and have nowhere to go. They convince us we cannot rise above any circumstance. They can occupy our minds, hearts, and souls by whispering lies. Rattlesnakes try to shatter our vision.

Rattlesnakes' venom can travel into our blood streams, and try to reside there because we are too afraid to move. Our Father shows us how to put things under our feet and how to operate under His command. Remember God is one call away, and we can dial our Big Brother, Jesus, and Our Father to not only remove the venom, but also, to crush all the rattlesnakes in our lives.

"God has put all things under authority of Christ and has made him head over all things for the church." Ephesians 1:22

Day Break

JOURNAL

Books from the Author

Lawanda N. Carswell

Daily Healing Words for the Soul

Day Break Devotions: 40-Day Journey

After the Storm - Vol. I

Day Break Devotions: 40-Day Journey

How I Got Over - Vol. II

(Coming Soon)

Day Break Devotions: 40-Day Journey

The Other Side of The Storm - Vol. III

(Coming Soon)

Mirror, Mirror...Reveals The REAL You

(Coming Soon)

www.ingramcontent.com/pod-product-compliance
Lightning Source LLC
Chambersburg PA
CBHW070445170726
48291CB00005B/1608

* 9 7 8 1 9 4 2 8 7 1 5 6 9 *